I wish I were...

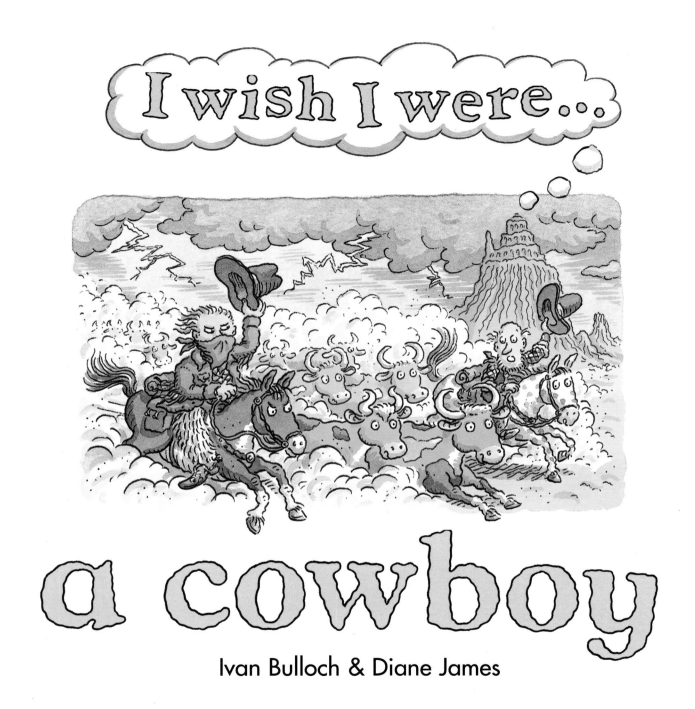

a cowboy

Ivan Bulloch & Diane James

World Book

Published in the United States by
World Book, Inc.
525 W. Monroe
Chicago, IL 60661
in association with Two-Can Publishing Ltd.

Art Director Ivan Bulloch
Editor Diane James
Illustrator Dom Mansell
Photographer Daniel Pangbourne
U.S. Editor Melissa Tucker, World Book Publishing
Models Ben, Jack, Matthew, Kelly, Eleanor,
Courtney, Kaz, Abigail

**Adult assistance may be necessary for some of the
activities in this book.**

**For information on other World Book products,
call 1-800-255-1750, ext. 2238, or visit us at
our Web site at http://www.worldbook.com**

Library of Congress Cataloging-in-Publication Data
Bulloch Ivan.
    I wish I were a cowboy/Ivan Bulloch & Diane James; [Illustrator,
    Dom Mansell; photographer. Daniel Pangbourne.] p. cm.
    Summary: Simple text and illustrations describe the life and work of
    cowboys and provide instructions for making such cowboy–related
    items as a vest, cardboard horse, lasso, and tent.
    ISBN 0-7166-5508-X (hardcover). — IBN 0-7166-5509-8 (pbk.)
    1. Cowboys—West (U.S.)—Social life and customs—Juvenile
    literature. [1. Cowboys.] I. James, Diane. II. Mansell, Dom, ill.
    III. Pangbourne, Daniel, ill. IV. Title.
F596.B92   1998
636.2 '13'092—DC21   98-20053

Printed in Spain

1 2 3 4 5 6 7 8 9 10 02 01 00 99 98 (hbk)
1 2 3 4 5 6 7 8 9 10 02 01 00 99 98 (pbk)

Contents

Cowboys of long ago had a tough, dangerous job looking after huge herds of cattle. They had to be strong, brave, and very good on horseback. There are still cowboys and cowgirls today, but life is a lot easier! Perhaps you would like to be a cowhand? *Are you ready for the ride...?*

Fancy clothes were no good for cowboys! They needed hard-wearing clothes that would last for weeks on end. Jeans were perfect. A hat with a wide brim kept the sun and rain off their faces. It could also be used to fetch water from a stream.

A leather vest was also useful because it left the cowboy's arms free when he was riding. The more pockets it had, the better.

1 To make your own cowboy vest, measure your chest with a tape measure or a piece of string. Then measure from your shoulders to your waist.

2 Cut a rectangle of brown paper slightly wider than your chest measurement, and as deep as your shoulder to waist measurement. Fold the rectangle as above.

Howdy, partner!

3 Cut two deep armholes and shape the neck. Use the drawing below to help with the shapes.

4 Decorate your vest using shapes cut from colored paper to make pockets. Use a felt pen to show stitching. Carefully put on the vest and ask a grown-up to tape the shoulders in place.

There was one thing a cowboy just couldn't do without—a scarf, called a bandana. He wore it to protect his face from dust and as a scarf to keep the sun off his neck.

The bandana could also be used for a knapsack, a handkerchief, or as a flag to signal danger. It could even double as a bandage or polishing cloth!

1 Here are three different ways to tie a bandana. First, to protect your face from dust. Fold a 15-in. (38-cm) square of fabric into a triangle. Tie the ends behind your head.

2 To protect the back of your neck, tie the ends of the triangle at the front. The piece hanging down at the back will keep the sun off!

Bet you can't guess what's in here!

3 To make a useful knapsack, lay the bandana on the ground. Put the things that you want to carry in the middle of the square. Knot together the ends diagonally opposite each other to keep everything in place.

In town, the most important person was the sheriff. His job was to keep the peace and make sure that any cowboys who happened to be around behaved themselves. If they didn't, they might end up in jail! The sheriff wore a large badge so there was no mistaking who he was.

1 Cut out a square of yellow or gold cardboard a bit bigger than the badge shape in the diagram.

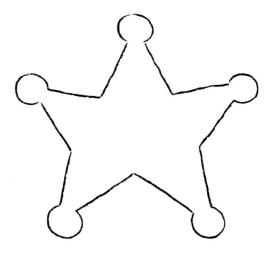

2 Copy, or trace, the badge shape onto your cardboard. To trace it, use tracing paper and a soft pencil. Turn the tracing paper over onto your card and draw around the shape again.

3 Cut around the shape. Use double-sided tape to attach the badge to your shirt or hat.

4 Just to make certain everyone knows who you are, you could write SHERIFF on the front of the badge before you stick it on!

A cowboy's best friend was almost certainly his horse! A strong, trusty horse could carry a cowboy for hundreds of miles, helping to drive the cattle.

Shake out your reins!

In return for this hard work it was a cowboy's duty to look after his horse at the end of the day. He had to rub him down, give him water, and make sure there was grass for grazing.

See you back at the ranch!

1 Find a cardboard box that you can stand inside. Ask a grown-up to cut out the top and bottom and make a slit at the front. You also need two holes on each side to run lengths of rope through.

2 Draw a horse's head on thick cardboard and ask a grown-up to cut it out, making a slit in the neck. Paint a mouth and eye on both sides. Glue on bundles of raffia or twine for a mane. Slot the head into the box.

3 Poke lengths of rope through the front and back holes to make a crisscross. Stand inside your horse and ask a grown-up to adjust the ropes to fit. Make knots on the outside to keep the rope from slipping through.

13

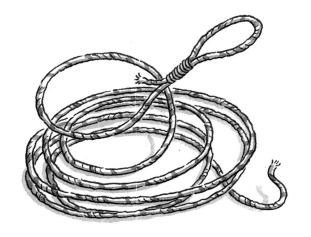

Ask any cowboy what his most useful equipment was, and he would reply, his lasso. This was a long rope with a small loop in one end. The other end slotted through to make a bigger loop. A skillful cowboy could throw the lasso over a runaway cow. But your lasso is just for show! Don't throw it around anybody!

1 Find a length of rope about 13 feet (4 m) long. Fold over about 4 inches (10 cm) at one end to make a small loop. Wind a piece of string around and around to secure the loop. Use tape to keep it in place.

2 Thread the other end of the rope through the loop to make a larger loop. Coil the unlooped end neatly.

14

3 You can carry your lasso over your shoulder, or attached to your horse's saddle. You should use it only for capturing cows!

oving cattle from the ranch to a place where they could be sold, thousands of miles away, was the main job in a cowboy's year. And the job was hard! A storm or sudden noise could frighten the herd into a stampede.

1 Ask a grown-up to help you cut out thick cardboard shapes to make the body and legs for your cow. Make thick slits as shown.

If it did, cowboys would race ahead of the herd, waving their hats and shouting, to try to turn back the leader and stop the stampede.

2 Decorate your cow by sticking on shapes cut from colored paper. Glue a length of rope onto the body to make a tail and shorter lengths to the top of the head for hair.

3 Slot the legs onto the body and your cow will be able to stand up. Now you will have to decide whether you have space to make a whole herd!

At the end of a long day, a good night's sleep was very important. If a cowboy was lucky, he had a tent for shelter.

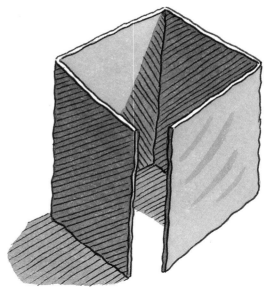

1 Find a large cardboard box. Try department stores that sell refrigerators and stoves. Ask a grown-up to cut off the top and bottom of the box and make a slit down one of the sides.

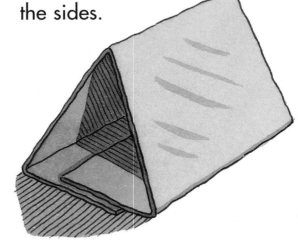

If a cowboy didn't have a tent, he had to roll up some of his clothes to make a pillow and sleep outside—with one ear open for cattle thieves.

2 Fold the box into a triangular shape. The overlapped edges make the base of your tent.

3 Cut a piece of burlap to fit over the tent. Ask a grown-up to help you sew or glue on felt patches. Drape the burlap over the cardboard frame.

Good night! Time for some shut-eye!

You can probably imagine how hungry a cowboy was at the end of a busy day in the saddle! Feeding hungry cowboys was no easy task. All the food had to be carried in a separate wagon, and it was mostly canned or dried.

No wonder cowboys looked forward to reaching town and a good meal!

1 To make a simple cowboy meal for two you'll need two large potatoes, some butter, and a can of baked beans.

2 Ask a grown-up to heat the oven to 375 °F. Scrub the potatoes to get rid of any dirt. Dry them and prick them all over with a fork.

4 Use a clean cloth to hold the hot potato and cut a cross on the top. Squeeze the potato to make a hole. Add some butter and spoon over the beans. There is no need to heat them, the potato will do that!

3 Bake the potatoes for about 1 hour. Ask a grown-up to poke them with a skewer to see if they are soft. If they feel hard, cook them a little longer. Put each potato on a plate. Open the can of baked beans.

Mmmm! That smells good.

O ne of the worst things that could happen to a cowboy was to have his cattle stolen! Cattle thieves were known as rustlers. Nighttime was the best time for them to attack, especially if they found a cowboy who had nodded off on his watch. Working quickly and quietly, they rounded up the cattle and galloped off before the cowboy could wipe the sleep from his eyes.

A cowboy's life was tough and tiring but exciting, too!